The 52-Week Stress Relief Journal

Welcome to The 52-Week Stress Relief Journal

This unique journal will give you 52 healthy and effective weekly activities designed specifically to help reduce stress and anxiety in your life. Plus, the specially crafted follow up questions will help support you in your journey and reinforce the positive progress and growth you're experiencing.

The reason this journal doesn't start on a fixed date is because neither does life. We all move at our own pace and time. Your commitment to reducing stress and anxiety in your life might not begin on January 1st. We all evolve and grow at our own pace throughout the year. Every 52-Week Journal is designed to work with you on your own time.

Whenever you're ready, so is this journal.

You can go in the order of the pages, repeat pages that specifically connect with you, or skip ahead to find new exercises and activities that speak to you where you are at any given time. It's all up to you! Positive mental health is about the freedom from life's many constraints. This journal's goal is to help inspire you to create a psychologically positive state of mind whenever you want.

As you'll see, most of the activities in this journal are designed to be done on your own. Others may be shared with someone special. You might find yourself reaching for this journal every day without fail. You might want to take the occasional break. With the 52-Week Journal you always set your own rules.

So, open up this journal, and open up your mind. It's time to recalibrate your life with all of the happiness and positivity you desire.

WEEK 1

Start an emotional vision board and add something to it every day that makes you feel relaxed and peaceful.

Pages from magazines, old postcards, even a sticky note with a handwritten thought on it all work when building a vision board. Choose any pictures, phrases or words that speak to you.

Date:_____

What were the first things you added to the board?

_____
_____
_____
_____
_____
_____

Did you hang the board somewhere you see it everyday?

_____
_____
_____
_____
_____
_____

Did you share the board with anyone?

_____
_____
_____
_____
_____
_____

WEEK 2

Think of a specific soothing thought or memory
to focus on any time you
begin to feel uneasy.

"Do not look for a sanctuary in
anyone except yourself."
~ Buddha

Date:_____

What special thought or memory did you choose?

_____
_____
_____
_____
_____
_____

Were there any stressful moments this week when you needed to focus on your special thought or memory?

_____
_____
_____
_____
_____
_____

How did you feel after focusing on that thought or memory?

_____
_____
_____
_____
_____

WEEK 3

Sit outside, get comfortable, and practice deep breathing every day this week.

Deep breathing increases oxygen flow to your brain and stimulates the parasympathetic nervous system, which helps promote the feeling of calmness.

Date:_____

Where did you choose to sit outside?

_____
_____
_____
_____
_____
_____

Did you feel more relaxed after deep breathing for a couple minutes?

_____
_____
_____
_____
_____
_____

Do you think you'll continue doing this regularly, perhaps in different locations?

_____
_____
_____
_____
_____
_____

WEEK 4

Write down three things you are grateful for and post that note in a place you'll see it every day.

Taking time to practice gratitude and reflect on things you're thankful for can lead to more regular positive emotions, better sleep, more compassion and kindness, and even building a stronger immune system.

Date:_____

What was the message on the card?

_____
_____
_____
_____
_____
_____
_____

Where did you hang it?

_____
_____
_____
_____
_____
_____
_____

How did it make you feel to see it every day?

_____
_____
_____
_____
_____
_____
_____

WEEK 6

Write down something that gives you stress or anxiety on a small piece of paper. Put the paper in a glass or metal bowl, go outside and (as safely as possible) burn the paper. While watching it burn, say out loud "You will no longer have power over me."

Nature has already proven that fire is cleansing, and new studies have shown that by simply believing in a personal physical reality you can actually push your mind and body to accomplish it.

Date:_____

What did you write on the paper?

_____
_____
_____
_____
_____
_____
_____

How did you feel while it was burning? And after it had completely burned away?

_____
_____
_____
_____
_____
_____
_____

Did you share the experience with anyone?

_____
_____
_____
_____
_____
_____
_____

WEEK 7

Set a strict bedtime for the week that allows you to get 8-10 hours of sleep. Wear a sleep mask so no light can sneak into your eyes.

Our circadian rhythm, the internal process that tells our mind when to sleep and when to be awake, craves consistency. Making an effort to go to bed in the same 20-minute window every night, and wake up in the same 20-minute window every morning, will train your body to fall asleep faster and easier.

Date:_____

What times did you go to sleep, and wake up this week?

_____
_____
_____
_____
_____
_____
_____

Did you set a specific pre-sleep routine to help you get ready for bed?

_____
_____
_____
_____
_____
_____

Did you notice any difference in your mood after getting more sleep?

_____
_____
_____
_____
_____
_____
_____

WEEK 8

Join a group exercise class.

Studies have shown that your mental, physical, and emotional quality of life is improved more during group exercise rather than solo exercise.

Date:_____

What kind of exercise class did you join?

_____
_____
_____
_____
_____
_____
_____

Did you make any new friends?

_____
_____
_____
_____
_____
_____
_____

Are there other group classes you would consider joining?

_____
_____
_____
_____
_____
_____
_____

WEEK 9

Mail someone a card with an optimistic message written inside.

Regularly sharing optimistic thoughts, and brightening someone else's day, can help you become more naturally optimistic.

Date:_____

Who did you mail the card to?

_____
_____
_____
_____
_____
_____

What did the message say inside?

_____
_____
_____
_____
_____
_____

What was their response?

_____
_____
_____
_____
_____
_____

WEEK 10

Add scents that you love to your office and home with a diffuser and essential oils.

Research suggests that citrus scents, such as bergamot, lemon, yuzu and orange, help alleviate stress and anxiety.

Date:_____

What scents did you try?

_____
_____
_____
_____
_____
_____
_____

What scent was your favorite?

_____
_____
_____
_____
_____
_____
_____

How did the scents make you feel?

_____
_____
_____
_____
_____
_____
_____

WEEK 11

Stroll through a lush outdoor space and make a conscious effort to admire the beauty around you.

Spending just 15 minutes per day outside exposes us to nature's vitamin D through sunlight, ideally protecting us from feeling sad.

Date:_____

Where did you go?

_____
_____
_____
_____
_____
_____

Did it make you want to go there again?

_____
_____
_____
_____
_____
_____

How did you feel afterwards?

_____
_____
_____
_____
_____
_____

WEEK 12

Give someone a hug every day this week.

A warm hug or snuggling up with a pet naturally releases oxytocin, the so-called "cuddle hormone" and increases serotonin, the "feel good hormone" into the body.

Date:_____

How did the hugs make you feel?

_____
_____
_____
_____
_____
_____
_____

How do you think they felt?

_____
_____
_____
_____
_____
_____
_____

Are there other people you want to try this with?

_____
_____
_____
_____
_____
_____
_____

WEEK 13

Have soothing music, or white noise playing in the background while you work.

Studies have shown background white noise can lower blood pressure, decrease heart rate, and increase relaxation as if almost in a meditative state without even realizing it.

Date:_____

What music or white noise did you choose to play?

_____
_____
_____
_____
_____
_____
_____

Did you notice a difference in your mood?

_____
_____
_____
_____
_____
_____
_____

Did you feel more productive?

_____
_____
_____
_____
_____
_____
_____

WEEK 14

Bring a pad of paper and a pencil to a museum or a beautiful park and draw the things that make you feel happy. Don't worry about what your art looks like, just keep drawing.

Focusing on creating art can put you into a "flow state" similar to meditation, where you become engrossed in an activity, distracting your negative thoughts and
lowering stress levels.

Date:_____

Where did you go to draw?

_____
_____
_____
_____
_____
_____

What things to you choose to draw?

_____
_____
_____
_____
_____
_____

Do you think you'll try this again in other locations?

_____
_____
_____
_____
_____
_____

WEEK 15

Listen to stand-up comedy or funny podcasts while commuting to work or school.

Laughing improves circulation and relieves tension in the body. Laughter also reduces the levels of stress hormones including cortisol and epinephrine.

Date:_____

What was the first thing you listened to?

_____
_____
_____
_____
_____
_____
_____

Did you find yourself laughing out loud?

_____
_____
_____
_____
_____
_____
_____

Did it make it feel like the drive went by faster?

_____
_____
_____
_____
_____
_____
_____

WEEK 16

Make your bed first thing in the morning every day this week.

Not only will you have already completed a task for the day, but science has shown living in a tidy environment improves focus, productivity, and lowers stress levels.

Date:_____

Did you feel better having already completed something for the day?

_____
_____
_____
_____
_____
_____

Did making your bed every day encourage you to tidy up anything else in your home?

_____
_____
_____
_____
_____
_____

Did if feel good to get into a nicely made bed before going to sleep?

_____
_____
_____
_____
_____
_____

WEEK 17

Clean out a closet, cabinet or drawer in your home or office. Make three piles - items to throw away, items to donate or give away, and items to sell.

Clutter can remind you of failures, distract you from getting things done and increase your levels of the stress hormone cortisol. Cleaning out clutter gives a sense of control over your environment and creates a calming effect.

Date:_____

What did you clean out?

_____
_____
_____
_____
_____
_____

Who did you donate items to? Did you make any money selling things?

_____
_____
_____
_____
_____

What else would you like to clean out next?

_____
_____
_____
_____
_____
_____

WEEK 18

Buy a bouquet of fresh flowers or a flowering plant and put it somewhere you'll see it every day.

One study showed that seeing flowers first thing in the morning increased happiness, gave a boost in energy and decreased anxiety.

Date:_____

What kind of flowers or plant did you get, and where did you put it?

_____
_____
_____
_____
_____

How did seeing, and smelling, fresh flowers make you feel?

_____
_____
_____
_____
_____

Does this make you want to add more flowers or plants in your life?

_____
_____
_____
_____
_____

WEEK 19

Drink a green smoothie every day this week. Add bananas, avocado or ginger for an all natural stress-busting punch.

Your daily diet is directly connected to emotional health. Eating raw leafy greens, ripe fruits and fresh veggies will feed your gut the nutrients that can help your clear your brain.

Date:_____

What was in your smoothies?

_____
_____
_____
_____
_____
_____
_____

Did you notice a difference in how you felt the rest of the day?

_____
_____
_____
_____
_____
_____
_____

Do you think you'll make this a regular daily thing?

_____
_____
_____
_____
_____
_____
_____

WEEK 20

Look through old photos and create a collage of your favorites.

Looking at cherished memories, especially amusing ones, elicits feelings of happiness and positivity and releases endorphins, which is our body's natural stress reliever.

Date:_____

When or where were the majority of the photos taken?

_____
_____
_____
_____
_____
_____

Did you hang the collage up somewhere it could be seen regularly?

_____
_____
_____
_____
_____

Did you share the collage with friends or on social media? If so, what was the response?

_____
_____
_____
_____
_____

WEEK 21

Binge-watch an entire season of a classic comedy show. Laugh all night long!

Laughter improves your mood and lessens anxiety by stimulating your heart and lungs, aiding in muscle relaxation and increasing the endorphins that are released by your brain. Laughter really is great medicine.

Date:_____

What show did you watch?

_____
_____
_____
_____
_____
_____

What were your favorite episodes, and why?

_____
_____
_____
_____
_____
_____

How did you feel after watching it?

_____
_____
_____
_____
_____
_____

WEEK 22

Start or join a book club. Suggest reading books that are known to inspire and enlighten readers.

Not only are book clubs great ways to be social in an organized way, but research shows that reading for just six minutes can lower your blood pressure and decrease stress levels as effectively as other relaxation methods.

Date:_____

Did you start a book club or find one that already existed?

_____
_____
_____
_____
_____
_____
_____

What book are you reading?

_____
_____
_____
_____
_____
_____
_____

Have you found the book club conversations enlightening or engaging?

_____
_____
_____
_____
_____
_____
_____

WEEK 23

Take a hot bath with scented candles and listen to relaxing music. If you don't have a tub, a long hot shower can do the same thing.

Stress causes the muscles of the body to contract and tighten, so taking a hot bath can relax you physically and mentally.

Date:_____

Did the bath make you feel physically relaxed, emotionally relaxed, or both?

_____
_____
_____
_____
_____
_____

What candle scents did you use, and what music did you listen to?

_____
_____
_____
_____
_____
_____

Will you make this a semi-regular thing from now on?

_____
_____
_____
_____
_____
_____

WEEK 24

Start a puzzle.

Research suggests that focusing on a single task, such as working on a puzzle, can create a mental sense of tranquility by putting the brain into a meditation-like state.

Date:_____

What puzzle did you choose? How many pieces did it have?

_____
_____
_____
_____
_____
_____
_____

How long did it take to complete it?

_____
_____
_____
_____
_____
_____
_____

Did this inspire you to do more puzzles?

_____
_____
_____
_____
_____
_____
_____

WEEK 25

Print out a picture of you happy and relaxed and tape it to your bathroom mirror.

Studies have shown that having a positive self-image can boost our physical, mental, and emotional wellbeing.

Date:_____

What picture did you choose?

_____
_____
_____
_____
_____
_____
_____

How did you feel seeing that picture every day?

_____
_____
_____
_____
_____
_____
_____

Are there more pictures you now plan on framing or posting on the mirror?

_____
_____
_____
_____
_____
_____
_____

WEEK 26

Make a playlist of your favorite songs and sing out loud with them.

Studies have shown that listening to music will reduce stress.

Date:_____

What songs did you sing?

_____
_____
_____
_____
_____
_____
_____

Which one was your most favorite, and why?

_____
_____
_____
_____
_____
_____
_____

Was it fun and relaxing or did you feel silly?

_____
_____
_____
_____
_____
_____
_____

WEEK 27

On a clear night, find a place with very little ambient light, and lie down to simply gaze at the stars. Add a stargazer app to your phone to know exactly what you're looking at.

Stargazing can reduce stress by helping you put your emotions in perspective and reminding you that there is so much more in the universe than what worries you.

Date:_____

Where did you go to see the stars?

_____
_____
_____
_____
_____
_____

Did looking at the wide starry sky make you feel as if your problems are smaller than you think?

_____
_____
_____
_____
_____
_____

Did you share this experience with anyone else? Or want to do it again?

_____
_____
_____
_____
_____
_____

WEEK 28

Go to see a live performance of a play, musical, or concert.

Watching a live performance stimulates your senses causing brain waves to synchronize, creating a social bond.

Date:_____

What performance did you see?

_____
_____
_____
_____
_____
_____

How did you feel after going out?

_____
_____
_____
_____
_____
_____

Has this inspired you to see more live performances?

_____
_____
_____
_____
_____
_____

WEEK 29

Talk to your gut brain! Incorporate foods every day this week that contain the essential amino acid and tryptophan, to produce more serotonin. Salmon, eggs, cheese, spinach, pineapple, nuts and seeds all boost serotonin naturally.

A whopping 90% of serotonin, the body's natural "feel good" chemical that helps fight depression and anxiety and even helps you sleep better, is made in the gut, not the head.

Date:_____

What foods did you eat this week?

_____
_____
_____
_____
_____
_____
_____

Did you feel better after eating anything in particular?

_____
_____
_____
_____
_____
_____
_____

Will you add more healthy recipes to your daily diet now?

_____
_____
_____
_____
_____
_____
_____

WEEK 30

Write down three things you are grateful haven't happened to you.

A mental exercise called "negative visualization" may help rewire your brain to better appreciate what you already have,
but usually take for granted.

Date:_____

What were your three things?

_____
_____
_____
_____
_____
_____
_____

Did you share those thoughts with anyone else?

_____
_____
_____
_____
_____
_____
_____

Did it encourage you to think more positively?

_____
_____
_____
_____
_____
_____
_____

WEEK 31

Do something new and exciting – take art lessons, learn how to SCUBA dive, or train for a marathon.

Learning a new skill can have a direct positive impact on improving your self-esteem and wellbeing.

Date:_____

What did you do?

_____
_____
_____
_____
_____
_____
_____

Will you continue working on improving this new skill?

_____
_____
_____
_____
_____
_____
_____

Did this inspire you to try other new activities?

_____
_____
_____
_____
_____
_____
_____

WEEK 32

Choose an empowering quote you love and add it to your email signature.

"The greatest weapon against stress is our ability to choose one thought over another."
~ William James

Date:_____

What quote did you chose? Were there any you decided not to use?

_____
_____
_____
_____
_____
_____

Did anyone comment on it?

_____
_____
_____
_____
_____
_____

Did seeing it every time you sent an email inspire you?

_____
_____
_____
_____
_____
_____

WEEK 33

Build a strong feel-good tribe. Create a list of people that make you feel good and plan to spend more time with them.

Having healthy relationships not only reduces stress and anxiety, but can help you attain personal goals which has lasting effects on emotional well-being.

Date:_____

Who is in your new feel-good tribe?

_____
_____
_____
_____
_____
_____
_____

Did you set days and times to get together?

_____
_____
_____
_____
_____
_____
_____

Did you feel good just by creating your tribe and making plans?

_____
_____
_____
_____
_____
_____
_____

WEEK 34

Enjoy the sunset with a glass of wine or your favorite tea. Take time to really focus on the beauty of nature.

Knowing that the sun sets every single day, no matter where you are, gives you an organized way to get outside, relax your mind and take time to appreciate nature.

Date:_____

Where did you watch the sunset?

_____
_____
_____
_____
_____
_____
_____

What did you think about while you watched the sunset?

_____
_____
_____
_____
_____
_____
_____

How did it make you feel the rest of the night?

_____
_____
_____
_____
_____
_____
_____

WEEK 35

Choose your own mantra.

From thinking "no one can take your joy" to "you've got this" taking a few minutes to close your eyes, breathe deeply, and focus on your mantra can be a powerful anxiety reliever. Simply humming "OM" can boost nitric oxide in the body, helping to regulate your nervous, immune, and cardiovascular systems to increase blood flow and muscle relaxation.

Date:_____

What mantra, or mantras, did you choose?

_____
_____
_____
_____
_____
_____

How often did you use your mantra this week?

_____
_____
_____
_____
_____
_____

How did you feel after focusing on your mantra?

_____
_____
_____
_____
_____
_____

WEEK 36

Treat yourself to a special "Happy to You" gift for no specific occasion.

"Just when the caterpillar thought the world was ending, he turned into a butterfly."
Anonymous proverb

Date:_____

What gift did you give yourself?

_____
_____
_____
_____
_____
_____
_____

Why did you choose that particular gift?

_____
_____
_____
_____
_____
_____
_____

How has it made you feel to have it?

_____
_____
_____
_____
_____
_____
_____

WEEK 37

Try to cut back on caffeine this week. Slowly reducing your consumption over several days can help you change your habit without causing any withdrawal symptoms.

Although drinking some caffeine can have positive effects, too much caffeine can trigger the release of adrenaline, the "fight-or-flight" hormone, leaving you feeling more stressed or anxious than before.

Date:_____

How many days did you cut back on caffeine?

_____
_____
_____
_____
_____
_____
_____

Did you feel more clear-headed than you thought you would?

_____
_____
_____
_____
_____
_____
_____

Do you think you can make this a new way of life?

_____
_____
_____
_____
_____
_____
_____

WEEK 38

Make a date to do something social with a good friend, even if you don't think you want to. Open up, share your feelings, and take time to listen to how they are doing, too.

"The courage it takes to share your story might be the very thing someone else needs to open their heart to hope."
~ Unknown

Date:_____

How did it make you feel to share your feelings?

_____
_____
_____
_____
_____
_____
_____

Did you learn anything from the conversations you had?

_____
_____
_____
_____
_____
_____
_____

Were you surprised by how your friend reacted when you shared your feelings with them?

_____
_____
_____
_____
_____
_____

WEEK 39

Turn up the music and dance to your favorite songs. Dance like nobody's watching!

Not only will dancing improve your mood, but it can also fire up your endorphins and help you sleep better at night.

Date:_____

What songs did you use for your dance party?

_____
_____
_____
_____
_____
_____
_____

Did anyone else join in on the dancing?

_____
_____
_____
_____
_____
_____
_____

Did you get tired or invigorated? Did you feel better after all that dancing?

_____
_____
_____
_____
_____
_____

WEEK 40

Make your own healthy snack bars with ingredients such as oats, nut butters, dark chocolate, honey, and matcha powder.

Making your own healthy snacks is a one-two punch of stress and anxiety relief. Cooking is relaxing because it encourages creativity, and eating healthy snacks provides much needed nutrients to feed the brain and reduce stress hormones.

Date:_____

What snacks did you make?

_____
_____
_____
_____
_____
_____

Was it fun, or challenging, to make your own snacks?

_____
_____
_____
_____
_____
_____

Do you think you'll continue to make your own snacks more often?

_____
_____
_____
_____
_____
_____
_____

WEEK 41

Organize a game night with friends.

Playing fun games socially will increase levels of oxytocin and lower levels of cortisol in your body, both reducing stress and helping you sleep more soundly.

Date:_____

Who was part of the game night?

_____
_____
_____
_____
_____
_____

What games did you play?

_____
_____
_____
_____
_____
_____

Have you made plans to do it again?

_____
_____
_____
_____
_____
_____

WEEK 42

Go for a walk every day this week
and take lots of photos.

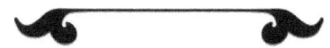

Spending time outdoors is widely known to
reduce stress and anxiety. Focusing on taking
photos adds to both the mindfulness of the walk
as well as creating calming memories.

Date:_____

Were did you go for your walk?

_____
_____
_____
_____
_____
_____

Did you invite anyone to join you?

_____
_____
_____
_____
_____
_____

What were some of the photos you took?

_____
_____
_____
_____
_____
_____

WEEK 43

Every morning this week, write yourself a note starting with a positive thought such as "I'm so glad I…" or "I'm the best at…" and leave it on your bed pillow to find every night.

Saying positive affirmations is a way to reprogram the subconscious mind and can make you less defensive or overwhelmed when presented with life's challenges.

Date:_____

What did your notes say?

_____
_____
_____
_____
_____
_____
_____
_____
_____
_____

How did you feel writing them every day and reading them every night?

_____
_____
_____
_____
_____
_____
_____
_____
_____
_____

WEEK 44

Learn to find and use acupressure points on your body. Combine this technique with simple self-massage on your feet and hands.

Engaging various pressure points such as between your eyebrows, on top of your feet and on your wrists can be used to instantly reduce anxiety and stress and may even help with insomnia.

Date:_____

What body parts did you choose?

_____
_____
_____
_____
_____
_____
_____

Did you feel relief or relaxation?

_____
_____
_____
_____
_____
_____
_____

Have you learned how you use any other pressure points?

_____
_____
_____
_____
_____
_____
_____

WEEK 45

Take a mini break to watch funny animal videos online.

"Always laugh when you can.
It is cheap medicine."
~ LORD BYRON

Date:_____

What videos did you watch?

_____
_____
_____
_____
_____
_____

Which ones were your favorites?

_____
_____
_____
_____
_____
_____

Did you watch any other videos that made you feel happy?

_____
_____
_____
_____
_____
_____

WEEK 46

Change the way you approach your to-do list so it's less overwhelming.

Try different methods, such as the Kanban Method or Pomodoro® Technique, that can give you a sense of achievement when completing tasks, and help keep you focused on only the most important items on your list.

Date:_____

What management systems did you try?

_____
_____
_____
_____
_____
_____
_____

Which one was the favorite, and why?

_____
_____
_____
_____
_____
_____
_____

Did you get more done or feel less anxiety using the method?

_____
_____
_____
_____
_____
_____
_____

WEEK 47

Plan a me-time vacation or day trip somewhere sunny.

Just the act of planning a trip can distract your mind from things that cause daily stress. Dreaming about where to go and what to do can release stress and lower tension.

Date:_____

Where did you plan on going?

_____
_____
_____
_____
_____
_____

Did you take steps to make the trip a reality?

_____
_____
_____
_____
_____
_____

Are there other trips you now want to plan on taking?

_____
_____
_____
_____
_____
_____

WEEK 48

Paint your walls a calming color.

Studies have shown that certain shades of blue, green and pink can help promote a peaceful atmosphere in the home and office. In fact, hospitals often use the a green or a blue/green color on both the walls and doctors' scrubs, due to its soothing response on the eyes and calming effects on the nerves.

Date:_____

What colors did you choose?

_____
_____
_____
_____
_____
_____
_____

What walls or rooms did you paint?

_____
_____
_____
_____
_____
_____
_____

Did you notice a different feeling in the atmosphere after changing the color?

_____
_____
_____
_____
_____
_____

WEEK 49

Spray lavender scented mist in your bedroom before going to sleep.

The scent of lavender may have the ability to soothe anxiety, help you fall asleep faster and encourage you to sleep longer.

Date:_____

Where did you spray the mist?

_____
_____
_____
_____
_____
_____

Did you notice you felt more relaxed in bed?

_____
_____
_____
_____
_____
_____

Have you thought about using other scents now?

_____
_____
_____
_____
_____
_____

WEEK 50

Create your own positive, inspirational quote, or
choose an existing one that really speaks
to you, and post it somewhere
you'll see every day.

"The mind is everything.
What you think you become."
~ BUDDHA

Date:_____

What is your quote?

_____
_____
_____
_____
_____
_____

Where did you post it?

_____
_____
_____
_____
_____
_____

How did the quote make you feel or inspire you?

_____
_____
_____
_____
_____
_____

WEEK 51

Make time to volunteer at a charity, pet rescue, library or other local organization.

By increasing self-confidence and igniting a sense of purpose, volunteering may reduce stress levels while enhancing your social network and creating meaningful
connections with others.

Date:_____

Where did you volunteer?

_____
_____
_____
_____
_____
_____
_____

How did I make you feel?

_____
_____
_____
_____
_____
_____
_____

Will you do it again? Or perhaps choose another place to volunteer your time?

_____
_____
_____
_____
_____
_____
_____

WEEK 52

Put a scrapbook together of all your favorite happy, stress-free moments.

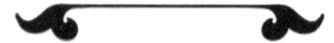

Scrapbooking is both creative and meditative while being emotionally heartwarming. And the best part is that you never have to worry about finishing it, you just keep making it better.

Date:_____

Looking back, did you have a favorite moment?

_____
_____
_____
_____
_____
_____

Did you show anyone the scrapbook?

_____
_____
_____
_____
_____
_____

Are there any favorite moments from this year you'd like to do again?

_____
_____
_____
_____
_____

PERSONAL NOTES:

Thank you for choosing us for your journaling experience!

Congratulations for completing the first steps towards creating the less stressful and anxiety-filled life you deserve.

If you enjoyed this journal experience, please check out the other versions we have at

www.52weekjournal.com

www.ingramcontent.com/pod-product-compliance
Lightning Source LLC
Chambersburg PA
CBHW020912080526
44589CB00011B/557